Yale's Hidden Treasures

Mystery of the Gothic Stone Carvings

Table of Contents

What a wonderful idea! The architect of Gothic Yale not only copied the solemnities of the style, but the carnivalesque nose-thumbing as well. Anyone who knows and loves Yale will have glimpsed a few of these — and here's a book that tells how they got there and why.

John Crowley
Senior Lecturer, Creative Writing
English Department, Yale University

I thoroughly enjoyed this well researched book that revealed the influence of religion on early education at Yale University. Interspersed with satire and humor, I found it to be a very entertaining and enlightening book.

Father John Poulos
(B.A. 1952)

I've walked through the Yale campus for years and was unaware of the scope and magnitude of the University's architectural design until I read this book. It's a fascinating and authoritative page turner filled with humor and compelling insight. Highly recommended reading.

Joel Vetsch
Actor/Producer/Director

Much of life is spent hurrying to our next appointment, or burying ourselves too deeply in our work that we do not take time to observe the beauty created around us, both natural and man made. This book walks us through the fascinating architecture and sculpture that is part of Yale's history and landscape. It illuminates the imagination and makes you wonder what stories the creators were attempting to tell the future generations of leaders that were to walk Yale's hallowed grounds. Take this trip with the author and photographer and feel free to make up your own stories and imagine mysteries that might have been.

Laurie Harkness, *PhD, CPRP*
Clinical Professor in Psychiatry, Yale School of Medicine

Preface

A hand-chiseled stone carving of a man with the head of a donkey, wearing a tuxedo, a bow-tie and tails, standing atop the law school roof of an elite Ivy League University...

Who could have thought of such a seemingly bizarre idea? Why are literally dozens of unusual stone figures found on several of Yale University's Gothic style buildings? How were they done, and more importantly, why were they done? Many of them are comical and appear to be done almost as an intentional joke on the part of the architect or the University itself. This might be the case if it weren't for the fact that each figure has a special significance associated with education at Yale. Still others are satirical, poking fun at various aspects of higher education and life in general. Over the years, Yale has been known for the "controversial" and some of these carvings echo that. How many people really know about them, and what do they know?

Another oddity is that many of these stone carvings are located on the high elevations of steeples and bell towers, while others are somewhat obscured by tree limbs. There are many smaller sized heads of Yale dignitaries that literally require binoculars to be seen from street level. Situated on the peaks of gables along the rear roof line of the Law Building are seven, three-foot high carvings of men with the heads of animals. These figures tend to blend right into the walls behind them, as all are made of the exact same stone. This part of the building, which gets very little sunlight, also makes these particular figures quite difficult to see from the sidewalk. It's as though the architect really didn't want some of these carvings to be easily seen. If so, why? Were they intentionally hidden in plain sight?

It's often been said "If these walls could only speak" or "I'd love to have been a fly on the wall" in reference to so many occurrences that have taken place in a room that years later people were never privy to. Many of Yale's stone carvings not only have ears but eyes as well. They also have mouths that unfortunately will never speak. One can only imagine all that they have born silent witness to over the past one hundred years since being hand chiseled in stone. They have heard future U.S. presidents and some of the greatest intellectuals of our time carrying on brilliant conversations as they strolled by these magnificent carvings. They have also witnessed some violent political demonstrations and riots that have taken place on the Yale campus during the turbulent 1960's. They will witness much more before turning to dust or being destroyed by future forces not yet known.

James Gamble Rogers, who has been described as stoic, had another distinct side to him. His alter ego came to life in the comical, satirical stone carvings that he created on Yale's Gothic style campus buildings. He never revealed why he created these carvings or what any of them meant. None of his other buildings were ornamented with the likes of such carvings. One could speculate that he intended for his stone carvings to carry on the Yale mystique that had begun with the formation of its secret societies years earlier and speculation gives rise to questions.

This book is devoted to the study of the stone carvings on the exterior of these buildings that face the street and the inner courtyards. It provides insight and information while presenting dynamic photographs of these intriguing figures. As revealed in subsequent pages, many of the stone carvings are far more than inanimate objects. Due to their satirical significance, they tend to take on a life of their own. Some of them are silently speaking to us with their own messages to convey. Many of them reveal stories of Yale folklore. With some curiosity and a little imagination, many interested passersby might be able to draw their own conclusions as to their real meaning. The history behind some of them may never be known. Indeed, the meaning of some may be left to the imagination of past, current and future generations. These masterful sculptures from a bygone era of stone masonry could be one of the University's best kept secrets and are part of what makes Yale so unique.

Acknowledgements

Sincere appreciation goes out from our entire book staff to Harold and Bobbie Miller, lifelong residents of the Greater New Haven area, for being instrumental in getting the book financed.

May I say that this book would never have been possible without the selfless support of Cheever Tyler (BA, 1959), and Dianne Pacl and Valerie Leri. *(Play with Grace, Sanctuary Productions)*. My respect goes out to the true professionalism of David Ross, our photographer and computer specialist, who worked tirelessly on this book for two years. My special appreciation to Yale University for cooperation and assistance. My gratitude to contributing photographer William Bartini of West Haven, Connecticut, on the Harkness Tower photographs.

Michael E. Stern

Forward

Yale has earned its reputation as a world-famous university. Its faculty is made up of scholars who are rich in knowledge and highly skilled in the art of teaching. The student body has always been made up of brilliant young men and women who are dedicated to scholarship as well.

A university of this stature would be entitled to take itself very seriously, and while Yale certainly does, it also has a sense of humor.

The stone carvings that are the subject of this fascinating book make it clear that Yale has always been willing to poke a little fun at itself. James Gamble Rogers clearly had a satirical sense of humor as evidenced by the clever stone carvings on his Gothic buildings.

Nonetheless, thousands of bright, inquisitive people have walked through the Yale campus over the years, and have not seen the stone carvings that look down on them. Michael Stern's book provides a clear view of Yale's stone carvings as well as their history. His book also teaches us that if we want to live full and fruitful lives, it pays to look up now and then.

Cheever Tyler, Esq. '59 BA

The Architect

James Gamble Rogers

James Gamble Rogers

Architect James Gamble Rogers designed several of his unique stone carvings for a very good reason. He thought they would be an ideal vehicle to convey, through the ages, his sometimes irreverent and comical views of education at Yale. Carved in the stone of the very buildings he designed on Yale's campus from 1917-1935, they are silent testaments to his architectural genius for as long as the University exists. A graduate of Yale in 1889, Mr. Rogers passed away in 1947 at the age of 80, yet in a way, he still lives on through his thought-provoking carvings.

The concept to create these stone figures and have them adorn Yale's newly built Collegiate Gothic style campus buildings was completely his brainchild and was in stark contrast to his strict architectural technique. As a Yale grad and the architect entrusted to design sixteen new buildings on the Yale campus, it may seem ironic to many that several of Rogers' carvings actually poked fun at Yale. One carving on the Sterling Law Building depicts a classroom in which the students are all sound asleep. A second carving shows a classroom in which the professor has fallen asleep. Should an Ivy League college have a professor who gives a lecture so boring that not only did he put a class full of disinterested students to sleep, he also put himself to sleep as well. Another carving in the hallway of Sterling Memorial Library shows a student reading a book with three large letters "U.R.A." on the left page and the large work "JOKE" on the right page.

Herein lies a scenario that has been quite difficult to uncover. Although the concept, design and meaning of these satirical carvings were entirely the work of James Gamble Rogers, they were all ultimately approved by the Yale administration. They were the vehicle he chose to help dispel the notion of many that Yale had an elitist attitude. He wanted to illustrate that Yale didn't take itself too seriously. This is not to say that there weren't dissenters within the Yale administration who objected to this approach, which did create some controversy surrounding these carvings. Are they not, however, in keeping with Yale's long tradition of liberalism laced with controversy?

His satirical barbs did not stop with Yale. The judicial system did not go unscathed. Several stone figures of participants in the legal process i.e.: lawyers, clients and judges are shown as well -dressed men with the heads of animals. One of the figures, a client, has the head of a donkey.

In the courtyard is a carved snail, representing the slow speed at which the legal process proceeds. In another scene, a law student sleeps soundly, his books piled high around him with cobwebs near his shoulders. Directly above a front door on the Law Building is a depiction in stone of a courtroom in which the judge is asleep.

There are also a few carved figures of workers who helped construct Yale's Gothic style buildings. One such carving is located on Davenport College. It shows a surveyor looking through a transit. Carved in stone beneath his figure is his name, "Sheff." Over the years, how many times have thousands of people strolled through this beautiful campus and wondered about who the builders were? These construction workers have long since passed on but at least the carving of Sheff, the surveyor, gives them an answer to their curiosity. On the other hand, James Gamble Rogers also designed many stone carvings of a serious nature, including full length figures of some famous and influential Yale alums such as Elihu Yale, Jonathan Edwards, Eli Whitney, Noah Webster, Samuel F.B. Morse, Nathan Hale, John Calhoun, and James Fenimore Cooper. These iconic stone statues exhort students to develop courage, truth and prosperity.

In 1917, Mr. Rogers began to design a complex on the Yale campus known as the Memorial Quadrangle that would define his career as well as the University's physical form for the rest of the Twentieth Century and beyond. With such newly introduced structural features as hand cut stone ornamentation, gable roof design, leaded glass windows, spires and slate roofs, this Collegiate Gothic style was to be Yale's architectural image from then on. It represented a major change in the campus' overall style. Exactly two hundred years to the day, after the first Yale building's cornerstone was laid, construction work began on the University's first quadrangle. It included Harkness Memorial Tower, the focal point of the campus and the tallest structure in New Haven at that time. Wrexham Tower, Branford College, Saybrook College, and five various sized interior courtyards, or courts, completed the Memorial Quadrangle. This magnificent fully enclosed complex was finished in 1921.

Harkness Tower is decorated with many hand-chiseled stone figures, some of a satirical/comical nature and some in a serious vein. Rogers' architectural style and philosophy was multi-faceted even though his work was also very serious and technically precise. His building design perfectly blended an urban and rural flavor. Celebrating the University's entire history, his campus buildings are full of tributes and references to Yale's location, where its founders came from, as well as its his charms, storytelling and wit, " Dean Stern pointed out. Clearly, the carvings revealed the light-hearted side of this architectural style. Another example of Rogers' "architectural wit" was his designing of Harkness Tower to be 216 feet high upon its completion in 1917, representing the 216 years since Yale's founding in 1701.

It is quite curious that James Gamble Rogers only placed four small faces on Wrexham Tower, located at the busiest intersection on the Yale campus. This would most certainly be the location where the greatest number of people would see his artistic carvings. It is even more curious that he designed many stone figures, the meaning of which are unknown to this day. They certainly are not generic carvings. There was obviously a specific reason that they were designed. No information has yet been found in Yale's archives.

Rogers left no known documentation about them in his papers or personal memoirs that we know of. Yale archivist and building curators do not know the meaning behind some of these figures. He conceived and created some of them completely aware that their meanings would never be known. It can be speculated that he wanted those who are curious about the meanings of these carvings to use their own creative imagination to draw their own conclusions. As is the case with abstract art, many people see different things in the same work of art. Higher education doesn't always give us the answer to a question, but rather it equips us with the knowledge to find the answers for ourselves. He knew that he had a massive Yale audience for his carvings. Graduate and undergraduate students alike, as well as faculty and staff members, encountered these works of art on the outside and inside of many Gothic campus buildings. The mystique of these carvings appeals to many Yale students regardless of their major course of study and to many alums irrespective of their various careers.

One thing is certain. James Gamble Rogers left an indelible mark on this University's campus and will always be an architectural icon at Yale!

The Sculptor

René Paul Chabellan
at work in his Manhattan studio

At work on-site at Yale University

and The Stonecutters

A stone sculpture of a stonecutter

A stonecutter at work

The Sculptor

When architect James Gamble Rogers finished designing each of his creative carvings, he turned to his long time friend, colleague and sculptor René Paul Chambellan to go forward with the project. Chambellan would use Rogers' drawings as his guide to hand make clay molds and three dimensional wood carvings. In turn, these materials were supplied to expert stonecutters, who hand chiseled Rogers' creations into and out of the stone on Yale's campus buildings.

In total, Rogers and Chambellan collaborated on over 150 of Yale's exterior and interior carvings, mostly in stone. René Chambellan worked out of his elaborate New York City studio and also on location at the job site. James Gamble Rogers' architectural firm was also located in New York, making their working relationship very logistically convenient. Both men made countless trips between New York and New Haven over a period of over twenty years.

A very well known sculptor of his time, Mr. Chambellan also completed many other building projects in New York City; Princeton, New Jersey; Michigan; Tennessee; Buffalo, New York; Chicago; South Carolina; and Cincinnati, Ohio. One of his more noted projects was sculpting the prototype for the Atlas statue in Manhattan's Rockefeller Center.

René Chambellan died on November 29, 1955 (at the age of sixty-two) of respiratory complications resulting from his service in World War I. He left behind a wealth of completed structural projects that bear testimony to his immense talent in the field of sculpture.

March 2, 1919

Photo courtesy of Yale archives

*T*his white plaster model, shown above, was made from a clay mold sculpted by Rene Chambellan. It was used to produce another mold that liquid metal was poured into, forming the figure of a mythical two-horned horse, pictured here. Its greenish tint indicates the metal had a high copper content. The liquid metal formation process was most likely outsourced to a local foundry. A metal smith on the construction staff then made the finishing touches to the figure and attached it to its stone cornice on the building. This figure appears with its identical twin on the upper building facade of Davenport College, facing the inner courtyard.

The Stonecutters

The ancient craft of stonecutting has been a closely guarded secret over the centuries. This technically demanding skill has mostly been passed down from father to son. Not taught in technical colleges or art schools, it is primarily learned through long apprenticeships. It is a technique that takes years to develop and perfect.

European countries in the old world best known for being a major source of stonecutters are Italy and Germany. Literally hundreds of stonecutters were brought over from these European countries to work on the massive construction project at Yale from 1917-1935. All sixteen of Yale's new collegiate Gothic style campus buildings, designed by architect James Gamble Rogers, were constructed during this eighteen year period. Many of these stone craftsmen required interpreters in order to communicate effectively with American construction personnel on site. Several of them ended up relocating in the New Haven, Connecticut area when the building project was completed and quickly assimilated into New Haven's ethnically diverse community. Many local middle-class working families would take in a stonecutter to help them pay their rent during the Depression Era.

The procedure begins with the architect's or artist's imprinted drawing of a carving being traced onto the stone to be carved as a starting point. The stonecutter is also supplied with either a clay mold or a hand carved, wooden three-dimensional model of the carving or statue. These prototypes are prepared by a sculptor such as René Chambellan. Before any hand chiseling begins, the stonecutter studies all of these materials supplied to him and formulates a mental image as to how he will next proceed. The stonecutters' implements were specifically made for shaping the carvings out of the limestone. This Indiana limestone was interspersed with the yellowish-tan colored seam-faced granite ashlar stone. Both types of stone were bonded together with mortar.

Primitive as it may seem, the three main tools used to carve out a stone figure are a hammer, chisel and a file. All are metal implements. The chisel is the instrument most critical to this process. Any metal chisel that is harder than the stone to be carved will effectively accomplish the purpose. The most commonly used chisel was made of forged steel. They had to be periodically sharpened during the process. It was an extremely tedious and time consuming procedure. Chisels and other stone cutting implements came in a variety of shapes and sizes required to achieve the correct detail. Liquid and dry finishing materials, such as sandpaper of various coarseness grades were used to smooth the edges and surfaces after the chiseling process was complete. Extreme caution and patience were obviously required. The total time required to complete a figure or statue depended upon its overall size and the amount of detail that the prototypes called for.

Completion times could vary from weeks to months. Obviously when working in stone, mistakes were very difficult to correct, so caution was the key word. With few exceptions, a carving was only worked on by one stonecutter. Typically, each stonecutter was assigned to do a specific number of carvings by himself.

All of the stone finials on the law buildings, such as the carvings of the men with the heads of animals, were hand chiseled on the ground, either on site or in a studio. They were then hoisted in position atop the roof and then cemented in place by use of pins at their base that fitted into corresponding holes drilled into the pre-selected roof position. Once the pins were cemented into the holes, the carvings became permanently in place. This is also the case with the eight iconic Yale figures positioned halfway up Harkness Tower.

Other exterior carvings of human figures and scenes were chiseled right out of the stone surfaces of building facades. A similar process was used in the case of all the owls appearing on the four towers of the law building auditorium. Each part of the owl was carved into a series of blocks that were then hoisted up, assembled, and cemented in position on each tower.

Even barring vandalism, these stone figures can be damaged and eroded over the years by the effects of weather and pollution. In 2009, the refurbishing of Harkness Tower began and took approximately ten months to complete. Several of the Tower's carvings required some re-chiseling and re-surfacing. Several stonecutters from Germany were brought in to do restoration work on these carvings. Specially trained and qualified contractors from as far away as Madison, Wisconsin were hired to undertake the refurbishing of one of the University's most sacred and symbolic buildings.

In the case of the original stonecutters, project assignments could run the full spectrum from several consecutive years of work to the same period of time without work. For most however, their trade was a "labor of love" which was a lifetime career and a way of life. The results of their talents and skills are preserved in stone through the ages. These stone masterpieces are absolutely awe-inspiring, as any observer strolling through the Yale campus can attest to.

The Buildings...

Harkness Tower

Sterling Law Buildings

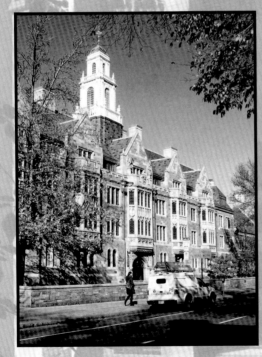

Davenport College

Sterling Library

and Their Carvings

Sterling Law Buildings

With stone carvings, leaded/stained glass windows, medallions and wood carvings adorning its interior and exterior, Yale's Sterling Law Building represents one of the finest examples of Collegiate Gothic architecture in the country.

The plan for a single building complex where law students could both live and study is modeled after the ideas of the English Inns of Court. Under the careful leadership of Yale Dean Thomas W. Swan (Dean 1916-1927), the plan came to fruition when the estate of John W. Sterling (B.A. 1864) made a gift of $5 million for the designing and construction of the Law Building.

Work began in August of 1929 with completion achieved in less than two years. Architect James Gamble Rogers' company from New York was the architectural firm. The builder was the Sperry and Treat Company of New Haven, CT. The entire concept of the carvings was the brainchild of architect James Gamble Rogers (B.A. 1889). The limestone figures and decorations were hand carved, while the handsome stained glass windows were designed by Henderson Brothers of New York. Frederick Kurtz completed the series of judicial medallions for the main staircase and the elegant wood carvings as seen throughout the building were created by the Irving & Casson-A.H. Davenport Corp. of Boston.

The building's design follows what is generally known as Collegiate Gothic. In this case, however, the architect quite freely included interpretations of Norman, early Renaissance and modern Gothic motifs. The building's design utilized limestone trim, part seam-faced granite, special-sized brick, steel casements, leaded glass windows, plus textured slate and copper roofs.

Extensive use has been made of symbolism in the sculptured stone and wood figures as well as in the stained glass throughout the school and dormitory areas. Included are scenes of judges and lawyers in costume; noted people connected with events of legal significance; officers of the Law; symbols of the Law; historical and modern instruments of the Law associated with the capture, trial and punishment of criminals; buildings associated with the Law such as the Inns of Court; symbols of Law and justice; and symbols of legal codes of all ages.

Many of the stained glass medallions were copied from illustrations in Les Cartes a Jouer, a book depicting the history of playing cards from the fourteenth to the twentieth centuries. The cards represent the game of life and all the aspects of human psychology. Greed, justice, love, war, hate, sorrow, passion and temperance are but a few of the many themes portrayed in these glass medallions. These all add to the flavor of humor, drama, whimsy and majesty of the Yale Law Building's architecture and decoration.

When campus tour guides bring thousands of tourist groups to this building each year, they encourage these fascinated visitors to look up, down and all around in order to experience and enjoy the treasures that the Yale Law Building offers. Although it consists of works of art produced by master craftsmen, the building is not a museum but rather houses functioning spaces for teaching, research, domicile and recreation.

The building's ornamentations are unique in their blending of different forms of creative design. They have been created to be enjoyed, used and cared for. Indeed, they are truly physical expressions of the philosophy and spirit of the Yale Law School.

15

Adding to the Gothic ambiance of the Law Building are four towers, each one rising from a corner of the auditorium. Each tower has eight owls carved into its stone surface. Through the positioning of several stone blocks containing the owl carvings, the owls' heads are three dimensional, whereas the owls' bodies are carved into the stone and flush with the tower's surface. This creates a visual effect that is quite unusual, as can be seen in the adjacent photograph. These owls are a metaphor that symbolize wise, nocturnal graduate students. No known significance has been found about the number of owls on the tower, other than they span the entire circumference of each tower.

Located in the ornate stonework about ten feet above the owls, are twenty-four small carved heads consisting of the faces of three different people. Each of the three peoples' faces is repeated eight times. These are the faces of middle aged Dutchmen, easily identified by their traditional hair styles and hats. These same faces appear on all four towers and are located about seventy feet above the ground. An observer would have to be looking for them with binoculars or through the telephoto lens of a camera to see them.

Apparently, architect James Gamble Rogers has left no information behind regarding the meaning of these faces, so it can be safely assumed that they are simply building ornamentation. Like most gargoyles, these types of generic stone figures are commonly found on the high elevations of many Gothic churches and public buildings in Europe. It is rather ironic that so many people pass by this beautiful building, yet so few people see them!

◀ A close up of the detailed carvings on one of the towers, The inset photo shows all four towers on the Law Building auditorium.

$\mathscr{A}$bove the Grove Street dormitory arch appears the figure of a Justice who has been blindfolded by a Court Jester wearing a cap with bells.

$\mathscr{A}$t the corner of the guest suites in the Grove Street court is the figure of an executioner with the head of a convicted criminal.

*A*top a buttress at the corner of York and Wall Streets is a figure of a gum shoe detective smoking a calabash pipe, wearing a derby hat and holding a magnifying glass.

A shield under a bay window of the auditorium, half way up the building on the corner of High and Grove Streets, shows a prisoner in stocks being reprimanded by a jailer.

Proponent & Opponent

The Puritan...

Religion was a major component of early education at Yale. Under a second floor window on the Grove Street side of the law building are two examples of finely detailed stone carvings. They both reveal the tremendous craftsmanship that these stone cutters possessed. One depicts a devout Puritan with religious book in hand.

and his Adversary

The other man, wearing the same puritanical garb, but having lost his hat, has obviously wandered from the straight and narrow. Although in front of a church, he is clutching a flagon of liquor in an inebriated pose. Surrounded by playing cards, a liquor bottle rests at his feet, while his smoking pipe sits in plain view. Clearly, the "slacker," who always avoids doing work, was one of architect James Gamble Rogers' favorite types of characters to portray in these stone scenes.

Rogers' Symbolic Courtroom Characters

A Lawyer as
a Wolf

A Lawyer as
a Bulldog

A Lawyer as
a Parrot

A Client as a
Goat with Money Bags

A Client as
a Donkey

Architect James Gamble Rogers chose these five symbolic stone figures to portray some of the participants in the judicial process. They are located high atop the gable ends of the auditorium near the corner of High and Grove Street. The architect specifically positioned them in close proximity because they are a group, with a common legal and biological bond.

Terra Cotta Heads

Policeman

Prisoner

$\mathcal{T}$his reddish-brown, hardened clay Terra Cotta substance is usually used on the surface of large buildings or made into small statuettes and vases. Using carved Terra Cotta heads to ornament the side of the law building is an architectural style not normally utilized.

Terra Cotta Heads

Lawyer

Judge

$\mathcal{T}$hese four symbolic characters are set in the stonework at the second story level on the High Street side of the building near Wall Street.

Stone Heads

Judge   Thief   Woman   Drunkard   Policeman

Traffic Officer   Murderer   Woman   Thief   Police Sergeant

These stone figures symbolize the varied personalities with which the law has to deal. Of all the carvings on the law building, these are the most widely recognized and remembered because they are located at the front of the building and remembered because they are located at the front of the building on Wall Street near York Street and are situated directly at eye level. The only unidentified figure is the woman, who could be either a witness or a victim.

$\mathcal{O}$n the stone cornice at the East end of the courtyards' North wall is a symbolic figure of a snail representing the slow speed at which the law works.

$\mathcal{O}$ver the entrance to the school section of the building in the main courtyard is found a stone carving showing Momauguin giving a deed of New Haven to Theophilus Eaton. In 1643, Momauguin (Chief of the Quinnipiac Indian Tribe) conveyed the deed for all of its land holdings to Eaton, a devout Puritan who represented a group of landowners. He was one of the founders of the New Haven Colony. This land extended from New Haven to Guilford, including a shoreline section of East Haven, later named Momauguin after the Indian Chief. The tribe sold this land for the same price in goods and trinkets as New Haven was sold for shortly thereafter.

Carving Representing
Doctor of Divinity

Carving Representing
Doctor of Law

*T*hese carvings appear on the upper corners of the Dean's Office large bay window at Wall and High Street.

*I*n the inner courtyard over the oriels on either side of the entrance to the school section of the building are two stone shields sculptured in the likeness of an Indian and a Puritan, Momauguin and Eaton.

$\mathcal{O}$n the corner buttress near the Grove Street arch over the entrance to the dormitory court is the stone figure of an Eagle, the United States' symbol.

*B*eneath the band course and fourth floor windows, the building has been ornamented with representations of a policeman's night stick, gloves & whistle and a motorcycle wheel.

The base of the balustrades on the Wall Street side are ornamented by a woolsack, a Judge's gavel and a Judge's wig. Few know that a clump of wool bound in a cloth sack, that came to be known as a "woolsack", was originally made for the English Lord Chancellor to sit on in the House of Lords. A woolsack was not only a symbol of his stature in the Court but it was also a means of physical comfort as sitting on hard wooden benches was quite uncomfortable after a few hours.

$\mathcal{T}$he figures of a square-toed shoe and a traffic light have been wrought in stone below the third floor window sills on Grove street. The square-toed shoe has been symbolic of the policeman walking the beat hour after hour, therefore coining the term "flat foot."

𝒜 stone panel beneath the third floor windows near the Wall Street entrance portrays an ordeal by fire. On the second floor level of the dormitory building facing the main inside courtyard is another stone panel that portrays an ordeal by battle.

$\mathcal{B}$etween the arches over the Law School entrance on Grove Street is a stone figure representation of Portia dressed as a man, posing as a Lawyer in the Shakespearean play, The Merchant or Venice.

𝒮ymbolic stone figure of an owl representing laws, above a large bay window, corner of Wall and High Streets.

$\mathcal{I}$n the stonework over the side entrance from the main courtyard to the lounge, a policeman is portrayed shooting at a thief.

$\mathcal{T}$here is a large stone figure of an English Judge at the west end of the inner courtyards' North wall.

*I*n the main courtyard, the figures on the North side buttresses of the dining room and lounge are, left to right, a law student, an English Judge, an American Judge and a Barrister of the 1850 period.

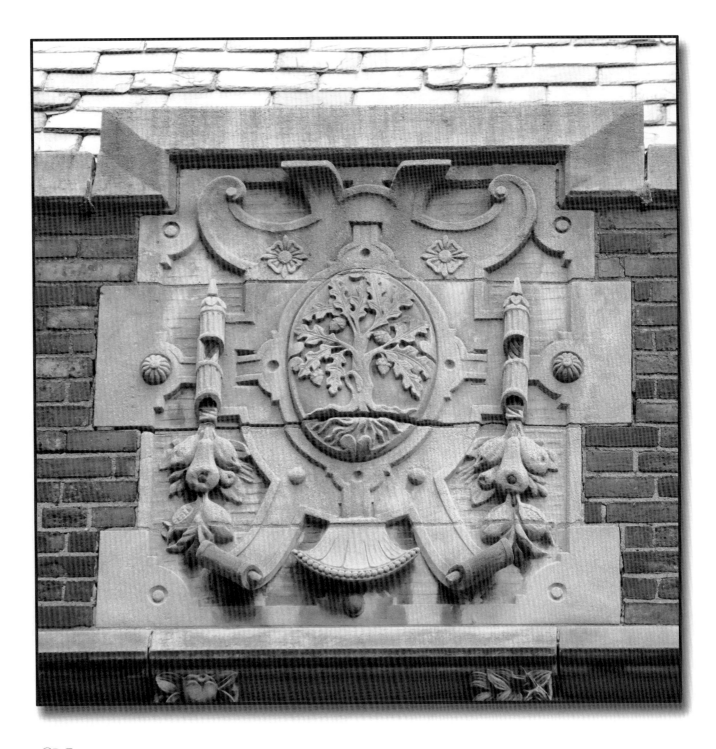

*T*he cartouche above the second floor windows of the distinguished visitors' quarters shows the famous Charter Oak.

*T*he stone figure of an ornamental Hebrew Scroll of Law appears above the doorway at the east end of the north wall.

𝒯he finial stone carving of a Judge as a bulldog can be seen rising above and in back of the visitors quarters roof.

$\mathscr{F}$igures done in lead on the top of a small tower on High Street near Wall Street are fashioned after Pegasus on his winged steed.

$\mathcal{L}$ocated on either side of the arch over the entrance to the dormitory court on Grove Street is a symbolic figure of the scales of justice wrapped in red tape. This is one explanation for why so many people feel that the "wheels of justice" turn very slow.

$\mathcal{I}$n the panel over the door between the High Street outer entrance and the vestibule, there is a scene in stone portraying a sleeping law student with his books and notes piled high about him and cobwebs around his shoulders. (Notice the opened liquor bottle with mice, spiders and an owl looking on.)

Some carvings have less detail than others because they were carved 1/8" into the stone, such as this carving, the classroom scenes and the police boat chasing the rum runner. The figures and finials, such as the men with animal heads, were carved out of stone and stand silhouetted against the sky or a building facade. These statue-like carvings are more prominent looking and have more depth, about 5". A few other carvings are noticeably pock-marked and weathered like the man with the initials AC on Davenport College.

Courtroom with judge asleep

Schoolroom with pupils asleep

*S*cenes over doorway leading from porch into Law School - Wall Street.

Roman Senator

Tribal Patriarch

$\mathscr{F}$raming the auditorium windows on High and Grove Streets are four seated figures.

Medieval King

Modern Judge

$\mathscr{O}$n the Vaulted Arches of the Law School entrance on Grove Street are symbols of a ball and chain plus handcuffs.

Laurel Wreath

Ball and Chain

Jailer's Ring and Keys

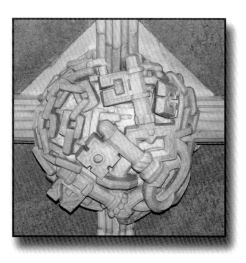

*I*f you look carefully at the symbols within the stonework on the vaulted arches of the main entrance, it will become clear what each of the items above are.

Judge Passing Sentence Upon a Criminal

Burglar on a Balcony

Policeman Apprehending a Burglar

Judge Passing Sentence Upon a Criminal

*O*n these five pages In the stonework of the Gothic arches at 127 Wall Street (main entrance) are figures symbolic of personalities within the legal system.

Convict in Stripes Contemplating His Crime

Convict Cracking a Stone

Lawyer as a Parrot

Policeman with a Club and Handcuffs

Burglar on a Balcony

Client as a Goat with Money Bags

One panel over the doorway of the Wall Street Court shows a patrol boat after a rum runner.

Harkness Memorial Tower

Architect James Gamble Rogers designed Harkness Memorial Tower to be not only the focal point of the Memorial Quadrangle but the focal point of the entire Yale University campus. Completed in 1921, the Tower rises to a height of 216 feet and was the tallest free-standing tower in the country at that time.

Named after Yale benefactor Stephen V. Harkness, who was associated with numerous people and activities involved in the University's history, as well as being a senior partner in John D. Rockefeller's Standard Oil Enterprises, Harkness Tower was intended to tie the new Memorial Quadrangle into the old campus on the other side of High Street. It was to be a symbol of Yale's unity.

The Tower rises upward by graduated stages, from the ground level War Memorial Chapel, to effigies of eight of the University's "most eminent sons." It continues upward to representation of life, progress, war, death, peace, prosperity, effort, order, justice, truth, freedom, and courage. Along the way, are located the subjects and people of an education in Western civilization, guarded by martial, business and professional figures. They are accompanied by the tag-along undergraduates and bulldogs. All of these stone figures symbolize that the Yale community has a powerfully charged relationship between the dead and the living. This is James Gamble Rogers' way of challenging current and future Yale generations to become the equal of its illustrious founders. This is the architect's and the Tower's Puritan sermon that was to ring out across endless time.

Harkness Tower has gotten its share of criticism over the decades for turning a perfectly good steel and concrete frame into a stage set as well as for its perceived "maleness" and authoritarianism. It has a softer side however. As the campus bell tower, its audible carillon bells playing dinner time melodies to all of Yale's students as they make their way to their residential college dining halls. Every afternoon and evening during the school year, a group of volunteer students ascends the stairs to the top of the Tower to play the 54-bell carillon.

As Yale students return to New Haven from all directions on the Connecticut Turnpike and Interstate 91, Harkness Tower can be seen from miles away, pointing the direction back to campus. When one visualizes the Yale campus, one visualizes Harkness Tower first and foremost.

Harkness Tower architect James Gamble Rogers placed Yale's most famous icons such as its benefactor, famous graduates and dignitaries on all four sides of this magnificent structure. He made them larger (8 feet tall) and placed them closer to ground level than the other figures. He wanted them to appear more prominent because they were more significant to Yale's history. The Tower was to display the University's treasured iconography like never before. They can be seen more easily from street level by viewing them through binoculars or a camera's powerful telephoto lens. Each of the eight stone statues was positioned in canopied niches atop the corner buttresses on both sides of the four clock faces. They are located about halfway up the Tower on the belfry. These eight notables appear in the following four photographs.

Jonathan Edwards. *October 5, 1703 – March 22, 1758*
(B.A. 1720)
> Greatest theologian and philosopher of British American Puritanism, stimulator of the religious revival known as the "Great Awakening," and one of the forerunners of the age of Protestant Missionary Expansion in the 19th century. Yale named a residential college in his honor.

Elihu Yale. *April 5, 1649 – July 8, 1721*
> Benefactor of Yale University for whom it was named in 1745. English merchant, official of the East India Company, he was buried at Wrexham in North Wales.

Noah Webster. *October 15, 1758 – May 28, 1843*
(B.A. 1778)
> Lexicographer famous for his American Spelling Book (1783) and his American Dictionary of the English language, 2 vol. (1828; 2nd ed. 1840). He was instrumental in giving American English a dignity and vitality of its own.

Nathan Hale. *June 6, 1755 – September 22, 1776*
(B.A. 1773)
> American Revolutionary War officer who attempted to spy on the British and was hanged without a trial. He is regarded by American Revolutionary tradition as a hero and a martyr. Minutes before his death he uttered the famous words for which he is so well known, "I only regret that I have but one life to lose for my country."

Samuel F. B. Morse. *April 27, 1791 – April 2, 1872*
(B.A. 1810)
> American inventor and painter who invented the electric telegraph (1832-35). In 1838, he developed Morse Code, a system for representing letters of the alphabet, numerals and punctuation marks by an arrangement of dots, dashes, and spaces.

Eli Whitney. *December 8, 1765 – January 8, 1825*
(B.A. 1792)
>American inventor, mechanical engineer and manufacturer, best remembered for inventing the cotton gin, but most important, for developing the concept of mass production of interchangeable parts.

James Fenimore Cooper. *September 15, 1789 – September 14, 1851*
>First major U.S. novelist. Author of the novels of frontier adventure known as the "Leather stocking Tales," featuring the wilderness scout Hawkeye. His most famous novel was "The Last of the Mohicans" (1826). His other novels included "The Pioneers" (1823), "The Prairie" (1827), "The Pathfinder" (1840), and "The Deerslayer" (1841). Although he studied at Yale, he never received a degree.

John C. Calhoun. March 18, 1782 – March 31, 1850
(B.A. 1804)
>A political leader as Vice President of the United States (1825-1832), a U.S. Congressman, Secretary of War, Senator, and Secretary of State. He championed states' rights, slavery and was a symbol of the Old South. Yale also named a residential college in his honor.

The ornamentation of Harkness Tower continues upward from the tier of Yale's eight icons. At a level slightly higher than the center of the clock faces (out from the 10 and 2 o'clock positions), on the center mullions of all eight belfry openings are the Greek figures of Phidias, Homer, Aristotle, and Euclid, representing the arts and sciences. Although these four did not attend Yale, it can be considered that they will exert a positive influence on Yale students. They are logistically in position to do so as directly above them are four grotesque birds representing the freshman, sophomore, junior and senior classes.

Further up on the clock face centerline are free-standing figures symbolizing business, law, medicine, and the ministry... the four fields of endeavor to which Yale students were traditionally called. At the same level, tied into the structure behind them, are three figures on each of the four buttressed corners. These twelve figures represent life, progress, war, death, peace, prosperity, effort, order, justice, truth, freedom and courage. Interspersed are figures of an education in Western civilization. They are guarded by martial and business professional figures, accompanied by tag-along undergraduate students and bulldogs. Included are eight representations of the characteristic soldiery or America's wars from the Revolution to World War I. A Revolutionary War soldier in a crouched position loads his flintlock; a sailor from the War of 1812 stands barefoot armed with his cutlass; a veteran of the Civil War looks down into the Branford College courtyard below and a sad-eyed soldier of World War 1 stands at attention, wearing his trench helmet.

Above these figures are eight small gargoyles, easily identifiable because they are the only horizontal elements on the Tower. They represent the four types of students: the scholar, the socialite, the literary man, and the athlete. It is interesting to note that the athlete is the only student with a happy expression on his face. These four student figures also represent the four classes of undergraduate students -- freshman, sophomore, junior and senior. Sharing the same upper level of the Tower are stone masks of Homer, Virgil, Dante and Shakespeare, each centered on a face of the octagon. At the same level, a small figure cowers at the feet of a stately Lady of Law. One of the abstract looking statues, wearing sandals, holds an eagle under one arm. Her other arm is cut off at the elbow, which is common in many Greek statues. Several statues of students are decked out in bow ties and rounded hats that were popular in the 1920's. It is very curious that features of some statues are not visible to observers on the ground, nor can they be easily seen from positions within the tower. Once again, "mystery adds to ambiance!" Rising above this level is the upper crown of Harkness Tower, comprising a full complement of detailed ornamental stone work. It certainly would not be an exaggeration to say that Harkness Memorial Tower is architecturally and aesthetically awe-inspiring. It stands as a further testament to the architectural genius of James Gamble Rogers.

East Side

(Facing High Street)

Elihu Yale

Jonathan Edwards
(B.A. 1720)

Lower Section

West Side

(Facing York Street)

James Fenimore Cooper

John C. Calhoun
(B.A. 1804)

Lower Section

North Side

(Facing Elm Street)

Nathan Hale
(B.A. 1773)

Noah Webster
(B.A. 1778)

Lower Section

South Side

(Facing Walkway)

Samuel B. Morse
(B.A. 1810)

Eli Whitney
(B.A. 1792)

Lower Section

East Side

(Facing High Street)

Upper Section

West Side

Facing York Street)

Upper Section

North Side

Facing Elm Street)

Upper Section

South Side

(Facing Walkway)

Upper Section

Top Students

The Scholar

The Socialite

The Athlete

The Literary Man

Eight horizontal carvings at the top of Harkness Tower represent four categories of student (the Scholar, the Socialite, the Athlete and the Literary Man). They also represent the four classes of undergraduate students -- freshman, sophomore, junior and senior. As these units protrude out four feet from the tower, they are partially secured by support wires that show in some of these photographs. Due to the weight of the stone, in time they could develop cracks and possibly break away from the tower.

The Supporting Cast

*I*n addition to the eight famous Yale icons, Harkness Tower is ornamented with numerous symbolic stone carvings. Located two-thirds of the way up the Tower are these three figures of people from different eras: A Revolutionary War soldier placed above the words "LEXINGTON 1775" (left); A nun carrying a jug of water, symbolizing religion (center); a stone statue of Euclid holding a tablet of numeric and geometric figures, representing the fields of art, science and mathematics (right).

The Supporting Cast

Rogers and His Assistants

On the ceiling of the foyer just inside the High Street entrance gate to the Memorial Quadrangle (1917), there is a group of four heads carved in stone. The head in the upper left photo is that of architect James Gamble Rogers. The other three heads are those of his assistants on the Yale construction project. The names of the three assistants are unknown.

Rogers' long time friend and colleague, sculptor Rene Chambellan, hand-carved three dimensional wooden models of these four heads in his New York City studio.

He used photographs of the men as a guide. A stonecutter would then carefully duplicate, in the stone carving, the depth and angle of each cut in the wooden model in order to achieve the desired detail. Upon completion of the four stone carvings, they were transported to the Memorial Quadrangle and carefully mounted on the ceiling.

It is interesting that each of the four heads were shown at different angles and that Rogers' name, as well as the names of his three assistants, do not appear with these heads. This just adds to the secrecy for which many of his carvings are known. It is quite obvious that he didn't want people to know the real meaning behind many of his carvings that were shrouded in mystery. Herein lies the mystique behind the stone carvings at Yale!

Davenport College

Directly across York Street from the west side of Yale's Memorial Quadrangle lies Davenport College, named after the Reverend John Davenport, co-founder of New Haven Colony and first to propose the establishment of Yale College at its present location. This residential college is one of a few "architectural contradictions" on the Yale campus. Architect James Gamble Rogers designed it to be a two-faced building, Gothic on one side and Georgian on the other. He equipped the outer facade facing York Street with height, materials, moats, stone-mullioned bay windows and leaded casements, similar to the Memorial Quadrangle across the street. The rear facade of the entry gate is unquestionably a version of Boston's Old State House, including a lantern tower and unicorns.

Architect James Gamble Rogers chose the exterior facades and roof cornices of Davenport College on York Street to place carvings in the likenesses of several construction staff personnel. Four notables, all with their names or initials carved next to their stone images, are Sheff (the surveyor), AC (a site planner), Drool (a scribe), and Art (a painter).

The "mystery carving" of a baby devil on the Roman philosopher's lap looking at each other, while a box with four crosses on it rests at their feet, remains officially unexplained. Although Rogers left no known explanation as to its meaning, which could have several implications, it can be conjectured that he was suggesting education and religion should peacefully co-exist, rather than be in adversarial positions. The meaning of several of his carvings such as two men reading their books and scrolls, located on both sides of the front entrance gate, are self-explanatory.

One of the most comical carvings on campus depicts a man riding a mule. It may or may not be intentional that the tie strings holding his hat on form the letter Y. It is unknown whether he was a worker on the project. Further down the building's facade is a stone owl wearing a graduation hat and tassle. He symbolizes the wisdom of a senior class student. One unusual feature of this owl is that he has bright yellow eyes. It is the only carving to have such a distinction. Nearby is a stone scene of a bulldog also wearing a graduation board, sporting bifocals and feverishly studying at his desk. He most certainly represents a senior student "slacker" who has procrastinated until the last minute before graduation to finish his senior paper, or thesis, as it was called back then. Two unicorns complete the various stone carvings on the outer York Street facade and are one of the few examples of generic stone images that architect James Gamble Rogers displayed on any of the Yale buildings he designed.

The only other figures on the building are twin mythical two-horned horses located on the courtyard side of the residential college. They are made of copper alloy material and are shown along with their descriptions in the following photo section.

"The Mystery Carving"

The specific meaning of this particular stone scene can only be conjectured. No known in formation has been found to date. As the University had ten founding Ministers, religion played a significant role in early education at Yale. This carving depicts a rapport between both factions, with the devil representing religion and the Roman philosopher representing education. The question becomes, to what extent? Notice the flames carved in stone behind the devil. May it be said that James Gamble Rogers wanted those who look at this carving to use their own insight and imagination when interpreting its mysterious meaning. After all, he attended Yale, his architectural client was Yale and those who teach and study here are in a constant quest for knowledge. Could this possibly depict a scenario in which an ancient religious philosopher, or mankind in general, is being tempted by the devil to do evil?

Readers at the Front Gate

These are two of only a few carvings on a campus building's exterior that are located at a hand's reach. As can be seen and felt, these limestone carvings are very porous and resemble cement. They are bonded to the seam-faced granite ashlar stone building using a special strong bonding cement containing traprock particles similar to the composition of concrete.

As most of the stone carvings and scenes on Davenport College are inter-related, their meanings are described in detail on the previous page. Photo captions in this section are brief vignettes.

Sheff the Surveyor

The Mystery Mule Rider with a Y Chin Strap

AC the Site Planner

Drool the Scribe

Art the Painter

A last minute thesis by a procrastinating senior Bulldog. A student slacker at his best.

$\mathcal{T}$hese twin mythical two-horned horses are located on the upper building facade of Davenport College, facing the inner courtyard. Mirror images of each other, they are examples of the very few metal figures that appear on Yale's Collegiate Gothic style buildings.

A Studious Owl with Bright Yellow Marble Eyes

Above the outside kitchen door at Davenport College facing York Street for all to see, but not to eat, is this stone carving of a cooked turkey on a serving platter.

Two Unicorns?

Guardians Year-Round

Sterling Memorial Library

$\mathcal{S}$terling Memorial Library is the largest library at Yale, containing over 4 million volumes. It is an example of Gothic Revival architecture, designed by James Gamble Rogers, and is adorned with thousands of stained glass panes created by G. Owen Bonawit. The Library has fifteen levels, each with its own category of books.

Rogers created the Library in the image of a Gothic Cathedral, even going so far as to model the circulation desk after an altar. He even required the Library to be seen from College street. As a result, Berkeley College was divided into two sections in order to create an unobstructed view of the Library.

The amount of stone transported for the construction exceeded the amount used, resulting in myths and legends on the campus that a fanciful structure existed on the roof, such as a miniature castle. The Library is named after John William Sterling *(Yale, 1864), who donated around $29 million to Yale upon his death. He was also a name partner in the New York law firm of Shearman and Sterling. Architect James Gamble Rogers remarked, "This library is as near to modern Gothic as we dared to make it." It is the great weight that shifted Yale's center of physical and psychological gravity from the old campus to cross campus.

Completed in 1930, the Library was featured in the 2008 George Lucas/Paramount film Indiana Jones and the Kingdom of the Crystal Skull. It appeared in the chase scene with Indiana Jones (Harrison Ford) and Mutt Williams (Shia Labeouf) escaping from pursuing Russians.

The Ancients

$\mathscr{I}$t is certainly no coincidence that Sterling Memorial Library would be ornamented with the stone figures of eighteen of the world's most influential scholars. Hand-carved statues of orators and pioneers in the field of education, philosophy, science, medicine, theology, mathematics and art, can be seen along both of the library's upper front facades, on either side of its High Street entrance.

The seven statues along the upper facade of the library's north wing are obscured by tree limbs and require extra visual effort to see. This ancient and cerebral iconology includes Socrates, Pythagoras, Homer, Plato, Aristotle, Hippocrates, Cicero, and Euclid. Mostly old world Greeks, the wealth of their knowledge and wisdom have been the subject of many a class-room lecture and term paper at Yale.

The Ancients

The Ancients

The Ancients

The Ancients

$\mathscr{S}$everal examples of multi-national lettering are carved into the stone façade above the main entrance to the Sterling Memorial Library. They include Hebrew, Egyptian hieroglyphics. Latin and Roman. These represent the main vehicle to educate by use of the written word, which is the primary function of a library.

𝓛ocated at the employees' rear entrance to the library on York Street is a carving depicting a Pilgrim and an Indian warrior holding their battle weapons.

The Potty Carving

$\mathcal{T}$his carving is significant for a few reasons, not the least of which involves a prank. This Puritan figure is sitting on a toilet pot on the peak of a second story roof at Trumbull College. Rather than facing the lower courtyard and Sterling Library, he is facing sideways instead. By facing away from the library, he is demonstrating the philosophical conflict between religion and early education at Yale.

In that freshmen are not allowed to live in any of the residential colleges, except Silliman, it is a Yale tradition that a member of the lower ranking sophomore class climb out onto the roof and paint the carving a different color each year. This year's chosen color is white. The court-yard directly below is aptly known throughout the campus, and Yale folklore, as "Potty Court."

Skull and Bones Initiation

At the end of the west interior courtyard of Trumbull College, above a wooden entryway door, is a series of scenes depicting initiation ceremonies into Yale's Skull and Bones secret society. Several hand chiseled figures representing the participants are horned devils, wolves, magicians, kings wearing crowns, Indians,clowns and puritans. Several of them are shown doing battle with each other. This is one of the few James Gamble Rogers carvings making reference to Yale's famous secret societies.

Skull and Bones Initiation

Courtyard Fountain

Located in the inner courtyard of Sterling Memorial Library is this composite of four hand carved stone gargoyles at the corners of a fountain. Derived from the word "Gargle", these gargoyles demonstrate one of their major functions which is to provide a water run-off as shown here.

Aphrodite and the Art Gallery Bridge

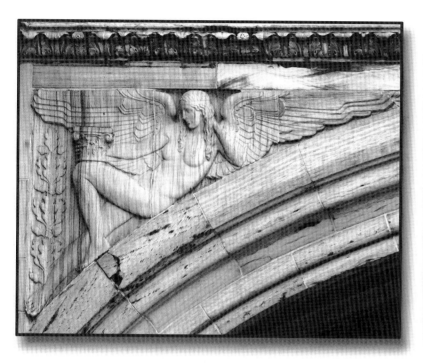

Aphrodite holding the top of an ornate Greek Corinthian pillar

Aphrodite holding a palate with paint brushes

Side of Arch Facing Harkness Tower

Architect James Gamble Rogers chose to ornament both sides of the Art Gallery Bridge with four carvings of a winged mythical Greek woman known as Aphrodite. Although she is the Goddess of Love and Beauty, Rogers wanted to associate her with art by depicting her nude and having the four carvings done on this arch. At the time of its construction in the mid 1920's, it connected the original Yale Art Gallery to the University's Art History School.

Aphrodite and the Art Gallery Bridge

Aphrodite holding a human torso

Aphrodite holding a man's head

Side of Arch Facing Chapel Street

Note: the vertical cracks running through the carvings resulting from almost ninety years of weathering.

The Missing Statues

The Missing Statues

It would seem that the mysterious meanings behind some of Yale's carvings are rivaled by several missing stone statues, conspicuous by their absence. Surrounding the main entrance to Sterling Memorial Library are seventeen vacant niches carved out of the stone walls, designed to house statues. In the main courtyard of Branford College, located in the Memorial Quadrangle, is an empty niche with the name Nathan Hale just below it. If missing, these statues would have obviously been pertinent to the University's prestigious history. The question remains why would this many niches be carved out if they weren't supposed to contain a statue? Empty niches look rather out of place as they currently appear on these buildings.

If one wishes to delve into this mystery for an answer, only a few possibilities can come to mind. One would be that due to poor planning, a last minute decision was made not to display any statues at all in these series of niches. Possibly there were originally some statues in them but after being removed for refurbishing, they were damaged and not replaced. If they were refurbished however, most likely the work would have been done while they were in place for the logical sake of ease and time. They are cemented in place and quite heavy, making it highly unlikely that a few people absconded with them in the dark of night. There are over a dozen vacant niches which would certainly seem to narrow down the possibilities.

Ironically, one of the missing stone statues has turned up not very far from its originally intended location. About halfway up Harkness Tower, the statue of Nathan Hale (B.A. 1773) can be seen standing in a canopied niche atop a corner buttress. Of course, there is still an identification problem because even if this statue is viewed through powerful binoculars, very few people would be able to tell who this statue is supposed to be. For the purpose of this book, it was identified from documentation in Yale's archives. Historical records do indicate, however, that most of these niches or "aedicules" were intended in the original renderings to be vacant. They are architectural design elements for ornamental purposes.

$\mathcal{O}$n the upper front facade of the Sterling Law Building auditorium facing Wall Street are five vacant niches. At the base of each niche is the head of a Medieval judge carved into the stone. Only the middle niche has an unmarked shield on its base. The identities of these judges are unknown. It is possible that a full length figure of each judge was originally intended to be housed in each niche. At the last minute, the architect may have changed his mind and decided just to carve the face of each judge into the base of each niche. We might also consider that these five niches were originally intended to be structured just as they appear.

$\mathcal{L}$ocated on the building facade of Branford College, facing the inner courtyard, is this vacant niche. The name of Nathan Hale(B.A.1773) is carved into the stone beside it. This niche was originally intended to house his statue. No more than 150 feet from this location, the full length statue of Nathan Hale can be found situated about halfway up Harkness Tower. The decision to include his statue as part of the eight Yale icons on the Tower was made after the original niche was prepared in the courtyard. It remains questionable why architect James Gamble Rogers didn't cover over Nathan Hale's original niche and name. One thing is certain, however. It clearly adds to the mystique of Yale's missing statues!

$\mathcal{O}$n the building façade of Branford College, facing the inner courtyard, is this vacant niche with the inscription "Scholar Athlete" carved into the stone next to it. One of the eight student gargoyles mounted at the top of Harkness Tower is described as an athlete and the only student bearing a happy expression As shown in the inset photo above, it is mounted on the Tower as a horizontal unit and therefor would not have been placed in a vertically shaped niche. Possibly at the last moment, it was decided that this figure would be shown as one of the eight horizontally mounted student gargoyles at the top of the Tower rather than having him appear as an upright figure in the niche.

Gargoyle Gallery

The Gargoyle Gallery

The word "gargoyle" seems to have different meanings to different people. It is defined in the Oxford English Dictionary as a grotesque spout, representing some animal of human figure, projecting from the gutter of a building in order to carry the rain water clear of the walls. It is derived from the word gargle, having to do with the throat. Some of these figures are grotesque looking creatures, half human and half animal, with horns protruding from their heads. Ironically, they are placed on buildings to ward off evil spirits even though they are evil looking themselves. Otherwise, they have no other meaning or significance. There is a fallacy that all of Yale's stone carvings are gargoyles. Nothing could be further from the truth! In point of fact, very few of the stone carvings that architect James Gamble Rogers designed are gargoyles.

Most people mistakenly think that they are strictly medieval because they appear on so many Gothic buildings. In point of fact, gargoyles have their origin in ancient Greek and Roman times.

In this section, we are presenting several of these "gargoylesque" figures, many of which appear on buildings other than those designed by architect James Gamble Rogers. Some are grotesque looking but none serve as drain spouts and none have satirical significance to education at Yale, as do many of the James Gamble Rogers carvings. They are simply interesting, generic building ornamentation's that have been carved in stone on Old Campus as well as on some other original buildings around the Yale campus. If they serve no other purpose, they certainly add to the ambiance at Yale. They exist to be observed and appreciated.

Gargoyle Gallery

Gargoyle Gallery

Gargoyle Gallery

Gargoyle Gallery

Gargoyle Gallery

Gargoyle Gallery

The Ribbon Cutting - 1930

Illustrations by Darell Koh
Storyboard by Michael Stern

Architecture of a Career

Self Portrait by Darell Koh

*B*orn and raised in Malaysia, twenty-two year old Darell Koh (B.A. 2011) is an extremely talented illustrator and cartoonist. Currently a senior at Yale University majoring in architecture, she plans to go on to graduate school to further her studies in this field.

Back home during her childhood years, Darell's mother strongly encouraged her and her siblings to draw, a skill that architects are required to have. She entered and won many drawing competitions. "I became interested in pursuing a career in architecture when I took a course in Urban Design my freshman year. I fell in love with the idea of cities." said Darell. After graduate school, she plans to work for an architectural firm in the United States.

Darell spent one of her summers in a Yale internship program called "Bulldogs Across America." She traveled to St. Louis, Missouri and started an urban community newspaper in the city's 21st Ward. "Cities like St. Louis are hidden gems that we unearth when working in their communities," she says. Darell has served as the Marketing Director for the on-campus Asian American Students' Alliance and Malaysian Singapore Students' Association "MASA." Darell has also done regular OP/ED illustrations for the Yale Daily News and the Yale Record. Some of her hobbies include photography and sketching scenes of cities and urban life. "I chose to attend Yale because of its strong Arts and Architectural programs. It's also really nice to be this close to New York City," she noted. This is certainly understandable as large cities tend to attract young, mature and talented individuals such as Darell Koh, who have a great work ethic and are dedicated to their craft.

Bibliography

MANUSCRIPTS AND ARCHIVES OFFICE, YALE UNIVERSITY

James Gamble Rogers and the Architecture of Pragmatism, by Aaron Betsky, pages 121, 126,132, 133, 137, 257, Ydl 994B.

Yale in New Haven, Architecture and Urbanism, by Vincent Scully and Paul Goldberger, pages 263-291, Yale University, New Haven 2004, Ydp 2004s+ .

Yale University, an Architectural Tour, by Patrick Pinnell, Princeton Architectural Press, pages 26-29,59-64, 69-71, 81-82, 97-98, Ydp 999P .

The Magic Pragmatism, the Work of James Gamble Rogers, from senior honor essay series by Paul Goldberger, record unit 118, series 2, box 1, folder 1.

Description of the Sterling Law Buildings at Yale University, Ydp 1, pages 18 – 21.

Wigs and Woolsacks, a Self-Guided Tour of the Yale Law School, Yale University publication, 1934, re-printed 1991, courtesy of Office of Public Affairs, Yale Law School, pages 1, 3-4, 5-19, 53-57.

Wikipedia, free online encyclopedia, feature article on sculptor Rene Paul Chambellan by Jim Patterson and Bob Perrone, July 2007.

The New Journal, the Magazine About Yale and New Haven, Volume 42, Number 3, from article "If These Stone Walls Could Talk", pages 16-17, November 2009, a Yale University publication.

Yale Law School: the Founders and the Founders Collection, a Yale Law library publication, number 1, Yale University Press, New Haven, June 1935.

Encyclopedia Britannica, 15th edition, volumes 2-5, 8, 12 for definitions.

The Oxford English Dictionary, second edition, 1989, for definitions.

The Inns of Court, by Cecil Headlam (with illustrations and paintings by Gordon Home, London, England, Adam and Charles Black, 1909.

Litchfield Law School, 1774-1833, by Samuel H. Fisher, biographical catalog of students, Yale Law Library publications, number 11, Yale University Press, New Haven, May 1946.

Background Information Provided By:

Father John Poulos, (B.A. 1952).

Dean Robert A.M. Stern, Yale University School of Architecture.

Mr. Amos G. Hewitt, Jr. , Hamden, Connecticut.

Mr. Bob Perrone, Allentown, Pennsylvania.